Food Chains

Julie Haydon

Contents

Rigby

Energy

Every living thing needs energy. Living things use energy to grow, move, and **reproduce**.

Living things get their
energy from food.

Plant Food

Green plants make their own food.

The sun's light, or energy, shines on the plant.

Green plants are **producers**. They make their own food using the sun's energy.

Green plants use the sun's energy, or light, to make their food. The green parts of a plant trap sunlight and use it to turn air and water into food for the plant. This is called **photosynthesis**.

Animal Food

This antelope is an herbivore.

Animals cannot make their own food. They must eat plants or other animals.

Animals that eat plants are called herbivores.

Animals that eat other animals are called carnivores.

This shark is a carnivore.

This racoon is an omnivore.

Animals are **consumers**.

They get their energy from eating plants or other animals.

Animals that eat plants and other animals are called omnivores.

Green Plants

Green plants are very important. If there were no green plants, there would be very little life on Earth.

Not all animals eat plants, but all animals depend on plants for their food. A zebra is an herbivore. It eats grass.

A lion is a carnivore. It eats animals
that eat plants, such as the zebra.

Food Chains

When plants and animals are linked by feeding, they form a **food chain**. Most food chains begin with green plants.

A food chain looks like this:

(is eaten by)   *(is eaten by)*

grass **zebra** **lion**

The arrows show how food, or energy, is passed along the chain.

Here are two more food chains.
They are longer.

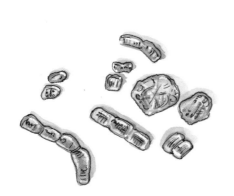

(are eaten by)

tiny water plants  **tiny water animals**

(is eaten by)

leaf **moth**

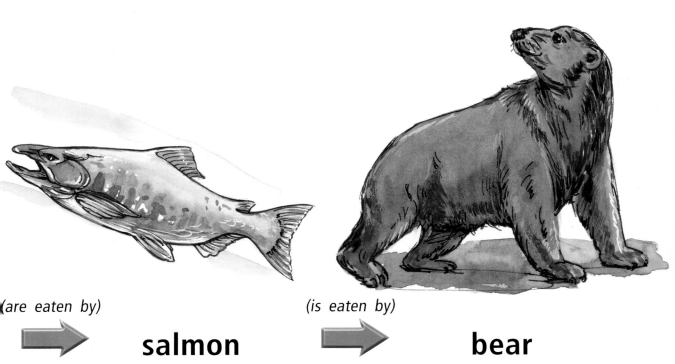

(are eaten by)

⮕ **salmon**

(is eaten by)

⮕ **bear**

**ȿ the salmon an herbivore
r a carnivore?** (See page 24 for the answer.)

(is eaten by)

⮕ **mouse**

(is eaten by)

⮕ **fox**

**the moth an herbivore
r a carnivore?** (See page 24 for the answer.)

There are always more plants than animals in a food chain.

Look at this pyramid.
If there were more
deer than plants,
the deer would
eat all the plants
and then starve.
Without the
deer to eat,
the wolves
would starve.

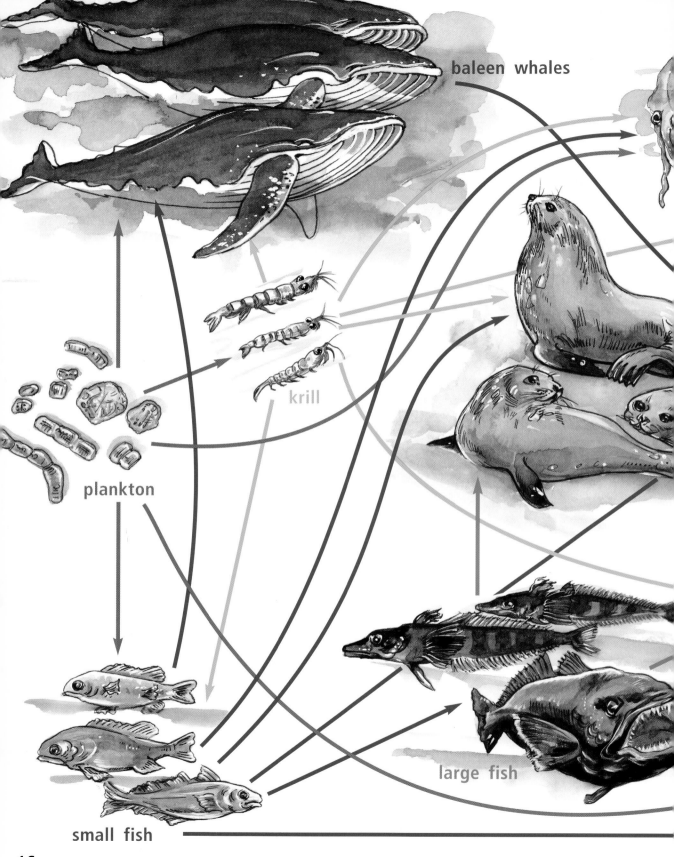

baleen whales

krill

plankton

large fish

small fish

Food Webs

In any **habitat**, most animals eat more than one type of food. This means that many food chains are linked together. This is a food web.

This is a food web in the Southern Ocean near Antarctica.

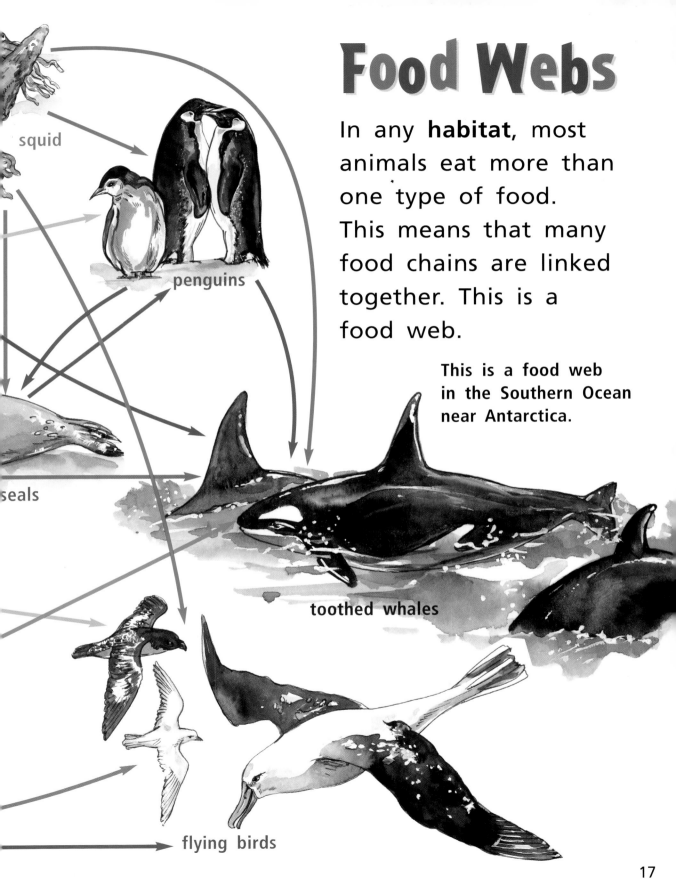

squid

penguins

seals

toothed whales

flying birds

Changing a Food Web

Everything in a food web is linked. A change to one type of plant or animal can make other changes to the food web.

Locusts are insects that eat plants. Sometimes, a **swarm** of locusts will fly to a new place and eat all the plants. Other animals that feed on these plants cannot find food. They starve.

The locusts are eating all the plants in the area.

People make changes to food webs, too. Changes can happen when people:

- Destroy habitats by clearing land
- Hunt too many animals
- **Pollute** habitats
- **Introduce** new animals or plants to a habitat

Catching too many fish will affect food webs.

Case Study—Whaling

Blue whales eat krill. Crabeater seals also eat krill.

Before whaling

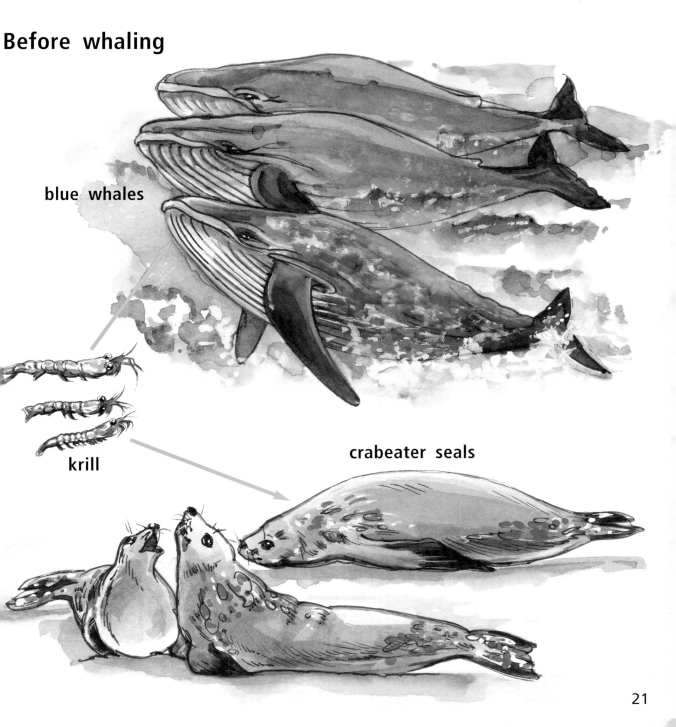

blue whales

krill

crabeater seals

When **whalers** killed lots of blue whales, the number of krill grew. With more krill to eat, the number of crabeater seals grew, too.

After whaling

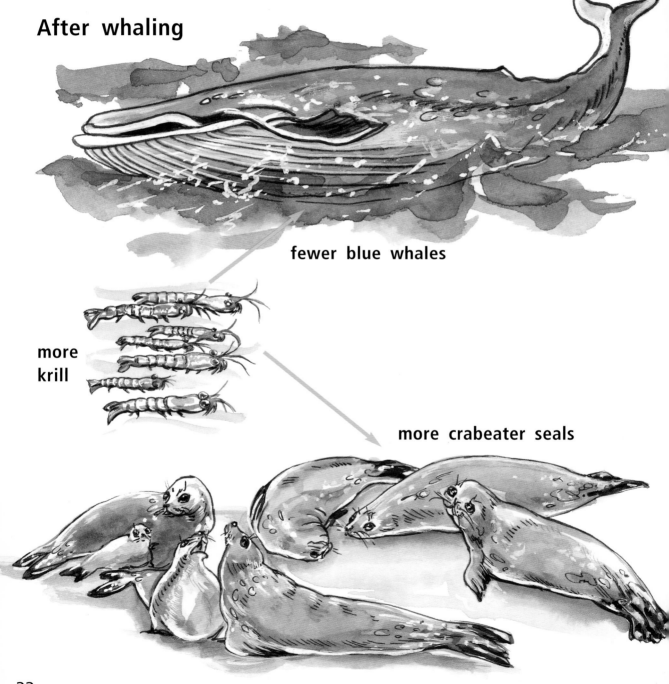

fewer blue whales

more krill

more crabeater seals

Food and You

Like all animals, you get your energy from food. Are you an herbivore, carnivore, or omnivore?

Draw a food web to show what you ate today. Include as many plants and animals as you can in your food web.

Glossary

consumers animals that eat plants or other animals

food chain a pathway or chain that shows how energy is passed from one living thing to the next

habitat the area where a plant or animal lives, feeds, and reproduces

introduce to bring into a place

photosynthesis the way green plants make their food from air and water using the sun's energy

producers green plants that make, or produce, their own food

pollute to make dirty

reproduce to have babies, or make the same species again

swarm a huge group of insects moving together

whalers people who hunt whales

Index

Page 13: The salmon is a carnivore. It eats other animals.

Page 13: The moth is an herbivore. It eats plants.

ANSWERS